IDLEWILD
the remote part

Guitar Tablature Vocal

The arrangements in this folio are intended only as interpretations of the recorded
works, rather than transcriptions. Standard guitar tuning has been used as
the basis for each of these arrangements, while some tracks were recorded
using the following tunings:

you held the world in your arms		C#, F#, C#, G#, A#, C#	capo 4
a modern way of letting go		C#, F#, C#, G#, A#, C#	
(I am) what I am not		C#, F#, C#, G#, A#, C#	
live in a hiding place		open G tuning	
out of routine	electric guitars	D, A, D, F#, A, D	capo 1
	other guitars	Eb, Ab, Db, Gb, Bb, Eb	
century after century	electric guitars	open G tuning	
	other guitars	Eb, Ab, Db, Gb, Bb, Eb	
tell me ten words		open G tuning	
stay the same		open G tuning	capo 3
in remote part/scottish fiction		open G tuning	capo 5

D1438591

Published 2002
© International Music Publications Limited
Griffin house, 161 Hammersmith Road, London, W6 8BS, England

Edited by Chris Harvey
Music arranged by Artemis Music Ltd
Artwork concept by R.Woomble. Art direction/Design by Traffic
Original cover image courtesy of The British Film Institute
Taken from the film *My Way Home*

you held the world in your arms

Words and Music by Colin Newton, Roddy Woomble, Rod Pryce-Jones and Bob Fairfoull

6

what if you held the world the world in your arms.

a modern way of letting go

Words and Music by Colin Newton, Roddy Woomble, Rod Pryce-Jones and Bob Fairfoull

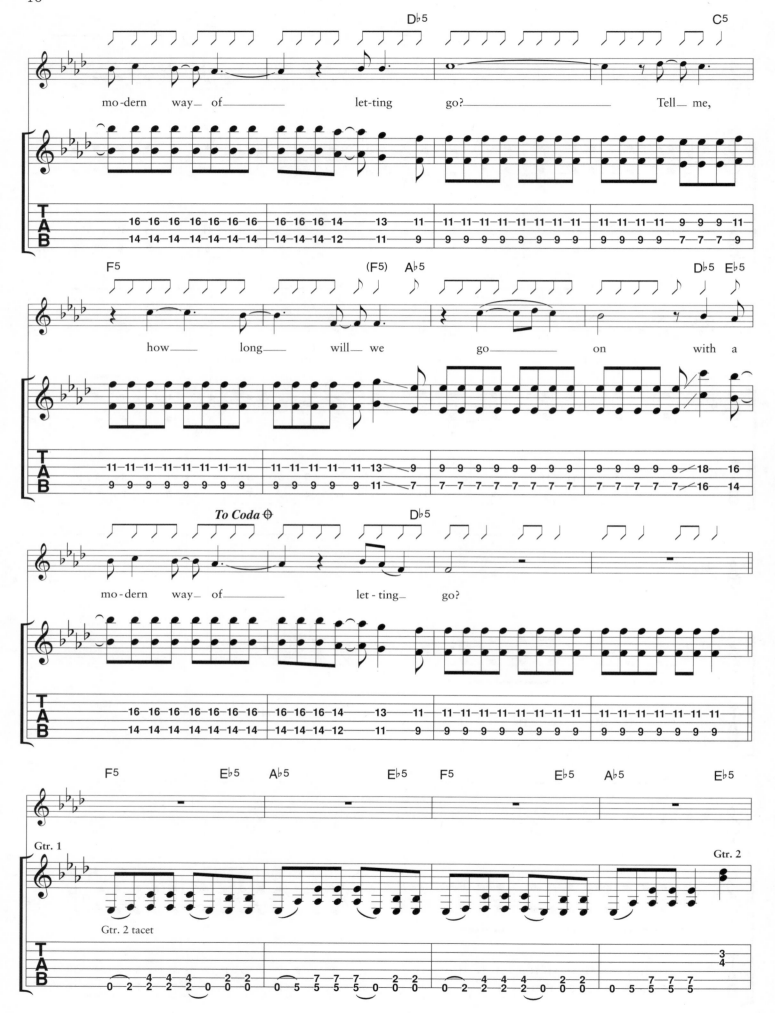

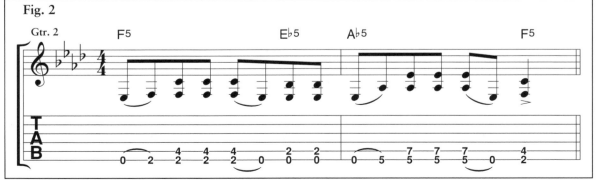

american english

Words and Music by Colin Newton, Roddy Woomble, Rod Pryce-Jones and Bob Fairfoull

19

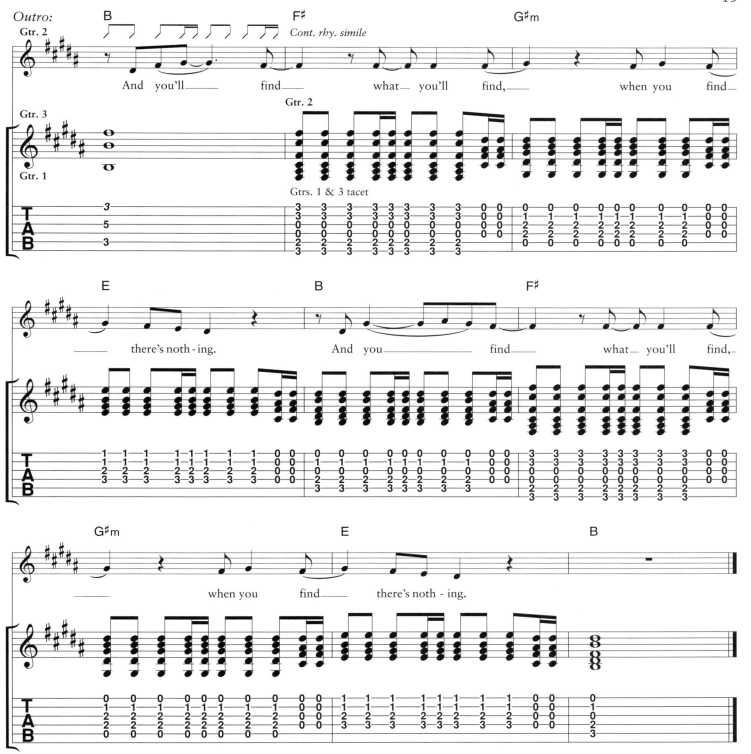

Chorus 2:
And you came along and found the weak spot
But you've always wanted
And let yourself be everything
That you've always wanted.

Chorus 3:
It doesn't have to be so decided
You've always wanted
No need for explanations
You've always wanted.

i never wanted

Words and Music by Colin Newton, Roddy Woomble, Rod Pryce-Jones,
Bob Fairfoull, Allan Stewart and Jeremy Mills

(i am) what i am not

Words and Music by Colin Newton, Roddy Woomble, Rod Pryce-Jones and Bob Fairfoull

live in a hiding place

Words and Music by Colin Newton, Roddy Woomble, Rod Pryce-Jones and Bob Fairfoull

32

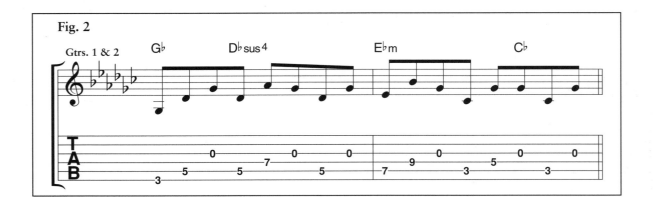

Fig. 2

out of routine

Words and Music by Colin Newton, Roddy Woomble, Rod Pryce-Jones and Bob Fairfoull

century after century

Words and Music by Colin Newton, Roddy Woomble, Rod Pryce-Jones and Bob Fairfoull

tell me ten words

Words and Music by Colin Newton, Roddy Woomble, Rod Pryce-Jones and Bob Fairfoull

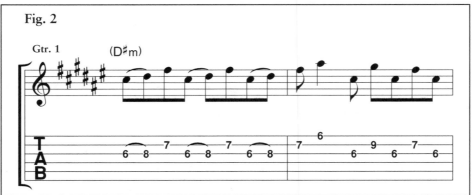

Fig. 2

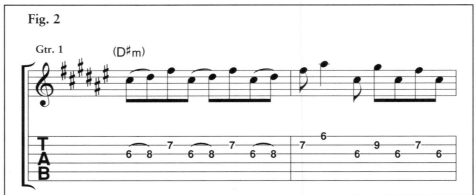

Fig. 2

stay the same

Words and Music by Colin Newton, Roddy Woomble, Rod Pryce-Jones and Bob Fairfoull

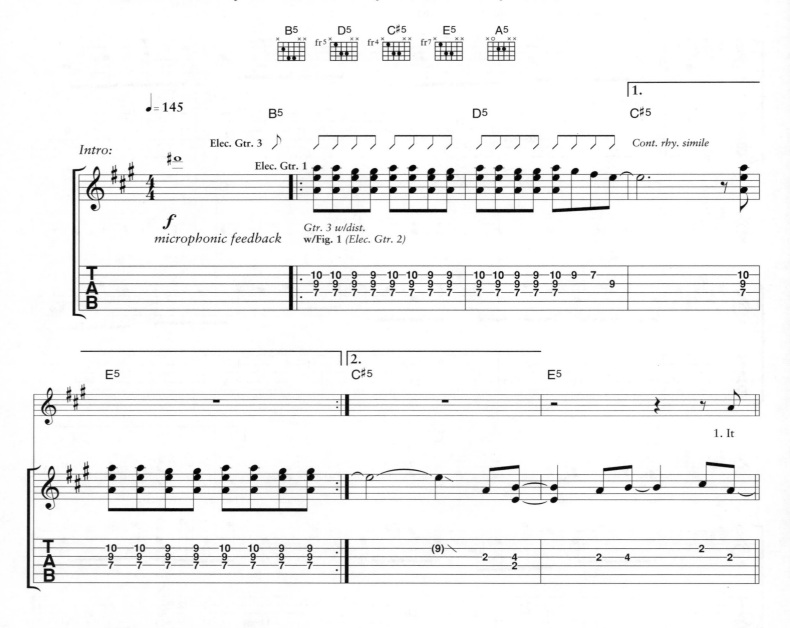

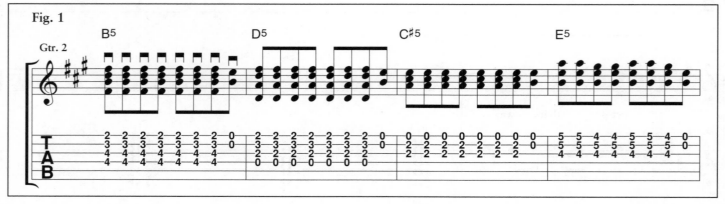

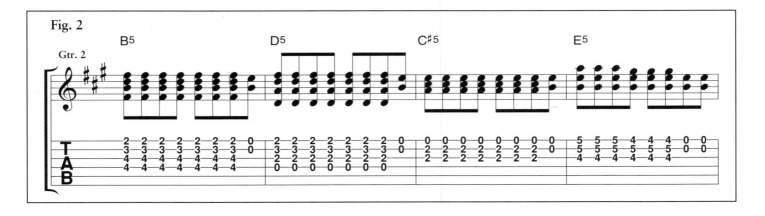

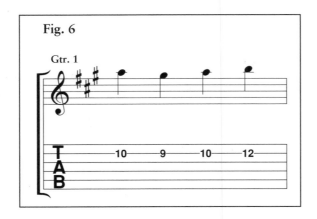

Fig. 5...

...Fig. 5 ends

Pre-chorus:

When I know— that   this won't sur - vive— much   long - er,   un-
And I know— that   what is— here   will not— be   here—

Gtr. 3 tacet
w/Fig. 3 (Elec. Gtr. 2) 2 times

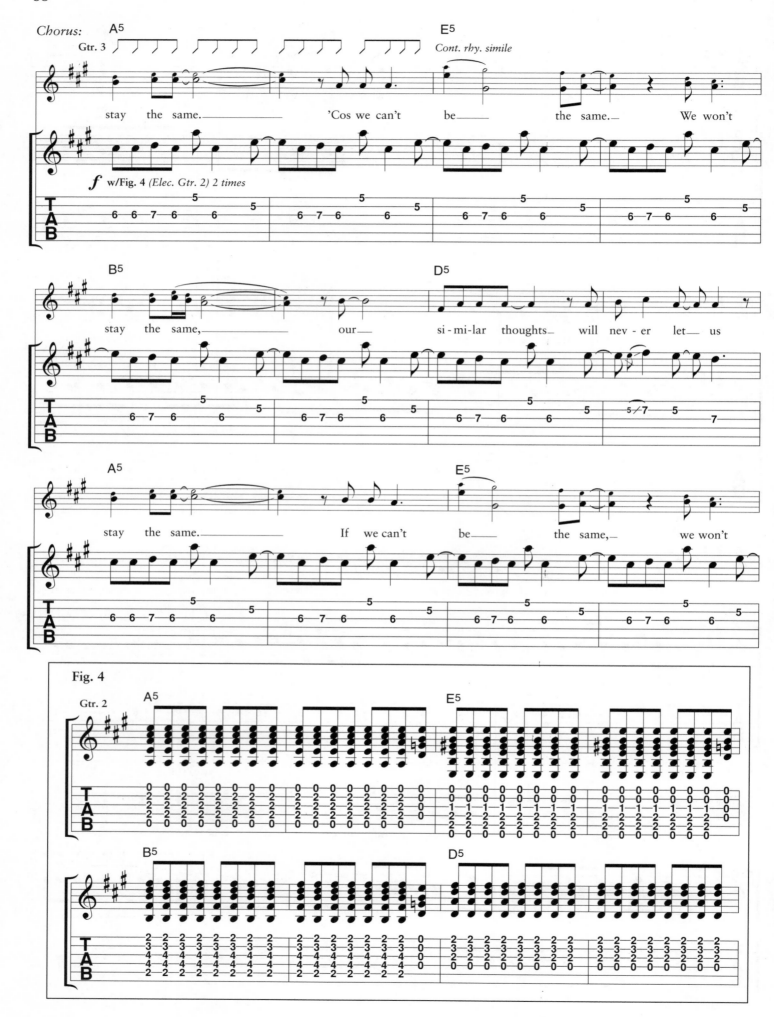

stay the same,_____ as we__ in - tend.____

_____ just be - cause___ we think__ we are___ the same.__

Solo:

w/Fig. 4 *(Elec. Gtr. 2) 4 times*

in remote part / scottish fiction

Words by Colin Newton, Roddy Woomble, Rod Pryce-Jones, Bob Fairfoull and Edwin Morgan
Music by Colin Newton, Roddy Woomble, Rod Pryce-Jones and Bob Fairfoull

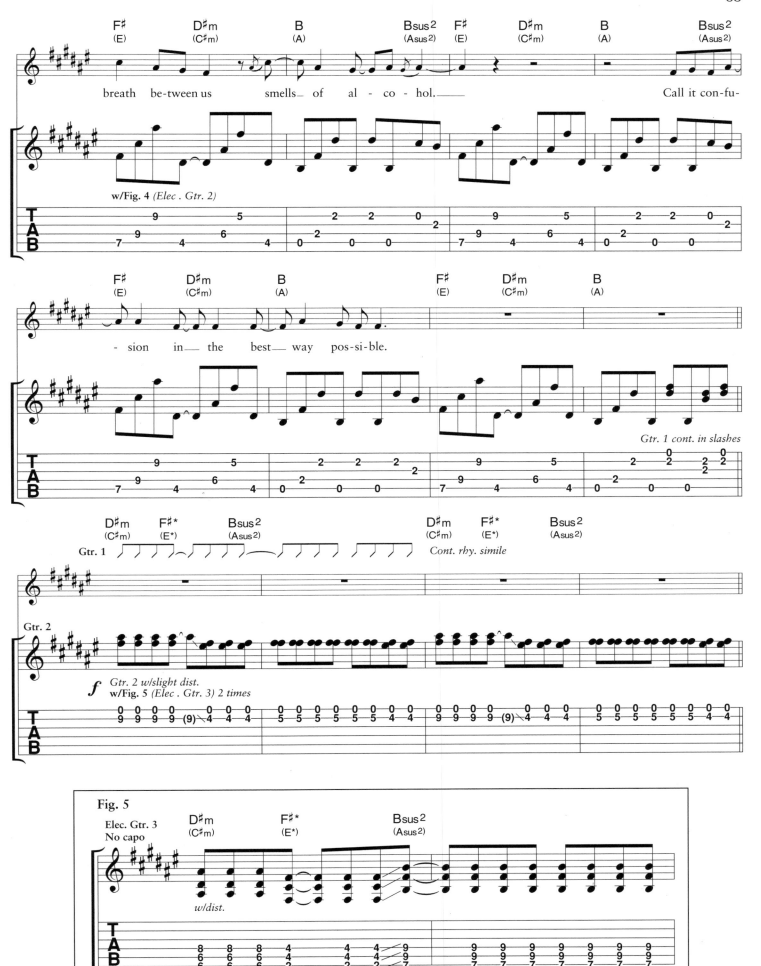

breath be-tween us smells_ of al - co - hol.____ Call it con-fu-

- sion in__ the best__ way pos-si-ble.

64

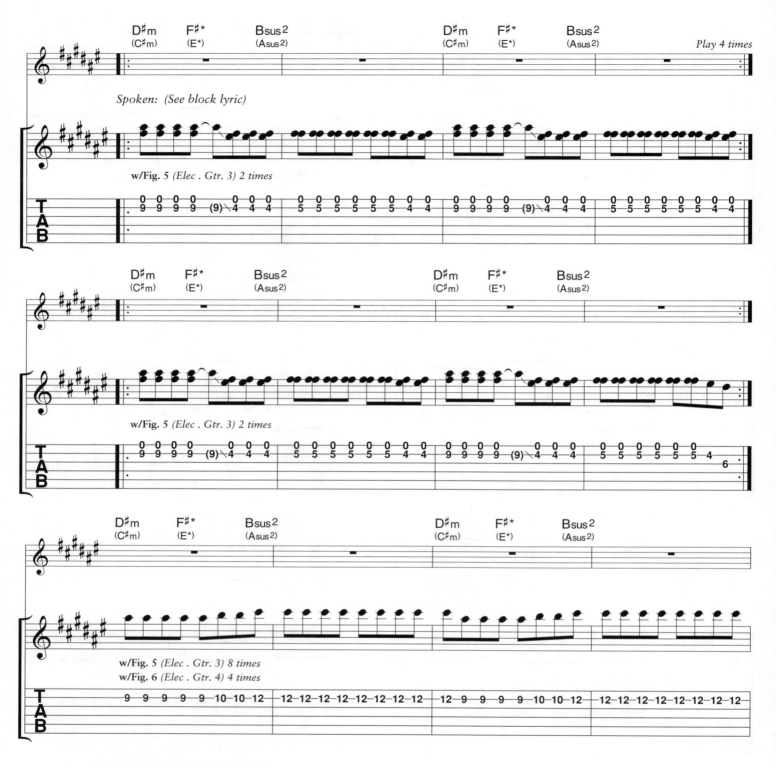

Spoken: *(See block lyric)*

w/Fig. 5 *(Elec . Gtr. 3) 2 times*

w/Fig. 5 *(Elec . Gtr. 3) 2 times*

w/Fig. 5 *(Elec . Gtr. 3) 8 times*
w/Fig. 6 *(Elec . Gtr. 4) 4 times*

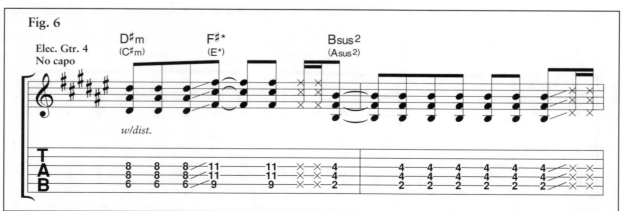

Fig. 6

Elec. Gtr. 4
No capo

w/dist.

Spoken:

It isn't in the mirror, it isn't on the page
It's a red hearted vibration
Pushing through the walls of dark imagination
Finding no equation
There's a red road rage but it's not road rage
It's asylum seekers engulfed by a grudge.

It isn't in the castle, it isn't in the mist
It's a calling of the waters as they break to show
The new black death with reactors aglow
Do you think your security will keep you in purity
You will not shale us off
Above or below.

Scottish friction, Scottish fiction.

Scottish friction, Scottish fiction.

Printed in England by Halstan & Co. Ltd., Amersham, Bucks.